Dad's Limericks

A collection of limericks he
wrote after age 90.

Compiled by: Johnny

Dad started writing these when he was in his early nineties. He was encouraged by his friend and caretaker Christi Hill. She also has input and wrote one or two of these herself. The best part about the Limericks are that he enjoyed writing them and sharing them to those he loved. I really loved listening to him tell them. He didn't read the limericks since he had every one of them memorized. As he would be sharing them, he would laugh and sometimes add a bit more to the limerick's story when it actually pertained to someone.

Dad wrote the one for his 92nd birthday during a visit my sisters and I enjoyed on Thanksgiving week in the middle of the pandemic in 2020. He was always one to button up loose ends and in his mind, having the final say was one of those loose ends. He would leave us on March 1, 2021 succumbing to cancer. He was 92 years young.

Thanks Dad for the memories and the limericks.

Johnny Reel

Dad's Limericks

Greedy

These people are not in need
Why do they have so much greed
Looking for someone for prey
It's the innocent they love to bleed

8-16-2020
About someone's estate that he wasn't too
thrilled of the outcome.

My Valentine

I will love you everyday
In a very special way
As my darling wife
You are the joy of my life
And you are here to stay

Do It

At ninety one I made a move
I had something to prove
To test my wit
And write a limerick
While I was still in the groove

New Toy

It's my birthday I am ninety one
Taking my four wheeler on a run
It's my new toy
For me to enjoy
And have some fun
    Christi Speaks

My name is Christi Hill

Caretaker for Carl Reel
He is such a nice man
And I will do the best I can
Utmost love and care is the deal

By Chris and Carl

Sweet Pea

Good morning sweet pea
Just how are thee
Did you come my way
To make my day
And be nice to me

Fine Cut

You are so special Darlene
The best hair stylist I've seen
You sat me in your chair
And did wonders to my hair
Which built up my self esteem

10-12-2020 by Carl Reel

Horny

I have a friend, Dick was his name
He did not hunt, women were his game
I tried my very best
To get him to take a rest
He died while loving his Jane

Smart Girl

She woke me up from my sleep
Wants to come up to clean and sweep
As she rushes up and down the hall
Cleaning my house wall to wall
Which is very neat

My Friend's Child

I met Chris when she was a child
When she was young and wild
Now that she is grown
She cleans my home
And does it with a smile

Susie

My personal banker Susie is the name
All bankers are not the same
I put her to a test
And she did it the very best
Best friends we shall remain

Smoke No More

How to quit that cigarette
Make someone a bet
Tell them you are going to quit
And then stick to it
You will have no regret

It's Love

I'm taking my pickup truck on a ride
With this lovely girl by my side
We lay on our blanket on the ground
And enjoy the love we have found
She's going to be my bride

Rowdy Friends

A few of my rowdy friends have settled
down
Most of them are buried underground
We the chosen few
Are trying something new
No partying this time around

Think

Think of every move you make
Please don't make a mistake
As you walk down the hall
Please do not fall
And you will have no bones to break

Cigarettes

Luckies were the name
But all are the same
He just had to have a smoke
Then he had a stroke
Oh what a shame

Frugal

Control how your money is spent
Do not spend every cent
Save some for a rainy day
And you will have you say
On where your money went

Mind Control

Control how your mind is used
Don't start singing the Blues
Never get in a hurry
And do not worry
About the bad news

True Love

You are so dear to my heart
I have loved you from the start
I will always be true
And never stop loving you
We should not be apart

Her Man

As he comes my way
I am hoping he will stay
He is a hunk of a man
And I have a plan
To make him mine someday

My Man

It is plain to see
He is the one for me
I would like to be his wife
For the rest of my life
And make him happy as can be

Covid 19

Will you please go away
We don't need you today
There is a problem with the virus thing
You have upset a beautiful spring
Please go and stay

Stay Home

My banker Susie called me
Said my money was safe as could be
And for me to stay home
Until this virus is gone
To this I will agree

Mother

I have made up my mind today
No more kids to come my way
I have four that I adore
Forgot diaphragm in dresser drawer
Later came pretty blue eyed Kathy Kay

DOB 10-10-1963

Finally

After all these years
He brought joy to my ears
He sat me down by his side
Asked me to become his bride
This brought me to tears

To Chris

My old towel was blue
I really loved it too
It was always hanging around
Now it can't be found
You hid it didn't you

Cane

Take along your waling cane
If you fall you will be in pain
As you stroll along step by step
Your cane will give you help
Fall and you are to blame

National Debt

I am worried about our national debt
Spending priorities have not been met
Liberals in Congress love to spend
This has always been their trend
And that leave me upset

Debt for Future Generations

The national debt of our fore fathers
Has to be paid by our sons and daughters
What were they thinking back then
To put us in the position we are in
To balance the budget is what matters

My Wife

My final search is done
I know I have found the one
To be my lovely wife
And enjoy a wonderful life
Loaded with lots of fun

Chris

You are just my style
Always with that smile
Staying in a good mood
And cooking fine food
You make my living worthwhile

Special Girl

She is one of a kind
That is hard to find
Please come my way
And make my day
And forever be mine

Waiting

I think of you everyday
In a very special way
I've been waiting a long time
For you to become mine
When is hard to say

Good Looking Man

When my good looking man arrives
He is not just one of the guys
He is nice as can be
And so special to me
There will be no more goodbyes

Bill was Best

Uncle Bill was in his prime
At his still making moonshine
Deputy fired at Bill on the run
Then dropped dead from Bill's gun
Bill go seven years jail time
       Note: Bill Lail son of John Lail

Carolina Moonshiner

My Grandpa Lail had many skills
One was making moonshine in the hills
He was making plans and thinking ahead
How his eighteen kids are to be fed
Why not make moonshine to pay the bills

Final

Writing Limericks for me and you
It's something I had to do
My album is now filled
And I am thrilled
Hoping you are too.

Inspiration and printing on original cards in his
album by Christi Hill.

Bye-Bye

It is plain to see
That she is leaving me
I could tell from the start
That I was not in her heart
Gone forever is very likely

Move On

Look at the trouble she has had
No wonder she is so sad
He screams and yells
Tell her to go to hell
I think he's going mad

Over the Hill

I just have this to say
There will be no more love and play
I am over the hill
And tried the pill
So you can go or stay

Waiting

I have waited so long
What did I do wrong
I have done my best
But I cannot rest
Until you come home

Impeachment Follies

President Clinton had just started his
second term
When he met a beautiful young intern
Later he had to confess
That he left upon her dress
Was his DNA tested sperm

Monica and Bill

Not too far from Capitol Hill
Monica is at the White House loving Bill
Watch out it's going on your dress
My oh my it's such a mess
Just for you to get a thrill

Hey You

If you have come to play
And I have my say
We will get out of town
And browse around
Maybe a romp in the hay

Greg Speaks

To her Dad I did not barter
She was going to be Vickie Carter
We played around
I knew I had found
The one to take to the altar

Together Again

Family came from far away
To see me on this Thanksgiving Day
Friendly chats and good food
Puts us all in a good mood
So thankful for their stay

At Ninety-two

At the age of ninety-two
What am I going to do
Just continue my way
Each and everyday
Or try something new

A former soldier, husband, father, funny, honest and good man wrote these Limericks in his early nineties encouraged by Christi Hill. He loved to share them to anyone that would listen and even those that didn't. I hope you enjoy them as well.

Carl Nelson Reel

February 20, 1929 – March 1, 2021

The photo on the next page is a truly representive of how he carried himself. He finished his career in the Army after two tours in Vietnam as a Warrant Officer II. This was a rank he was very proud to have achieved.

These pages have been left blank to
encourage the readers to write a Limerick
of their own and include it here on these
pages for all to enjoy.